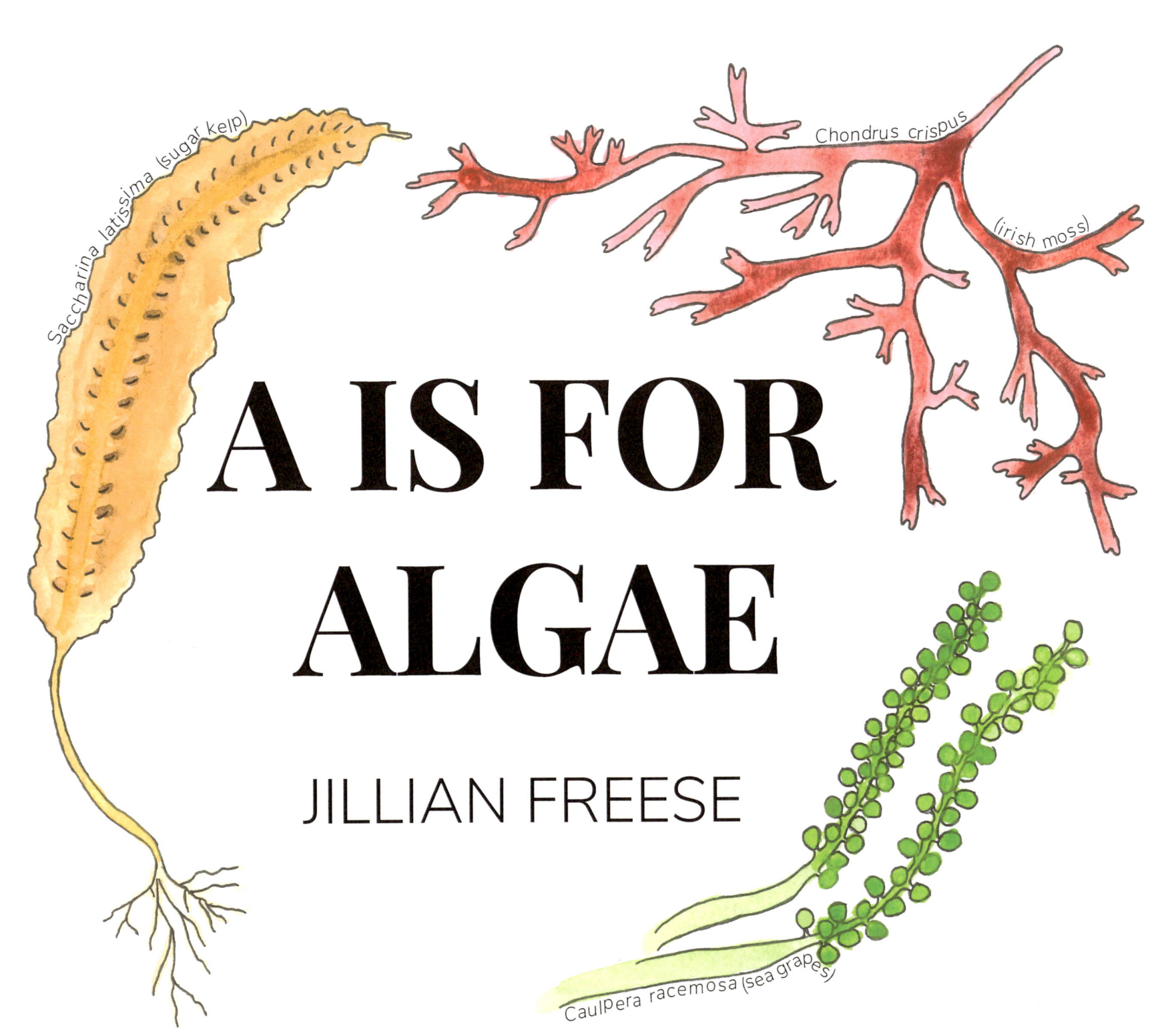

FOR
A. L. G.

A is for Alaria marginata

It's also known as winged kelp!

Brown Algae
Size: up to 13 feet/4 meters
Location: Northern Pacific Ocean

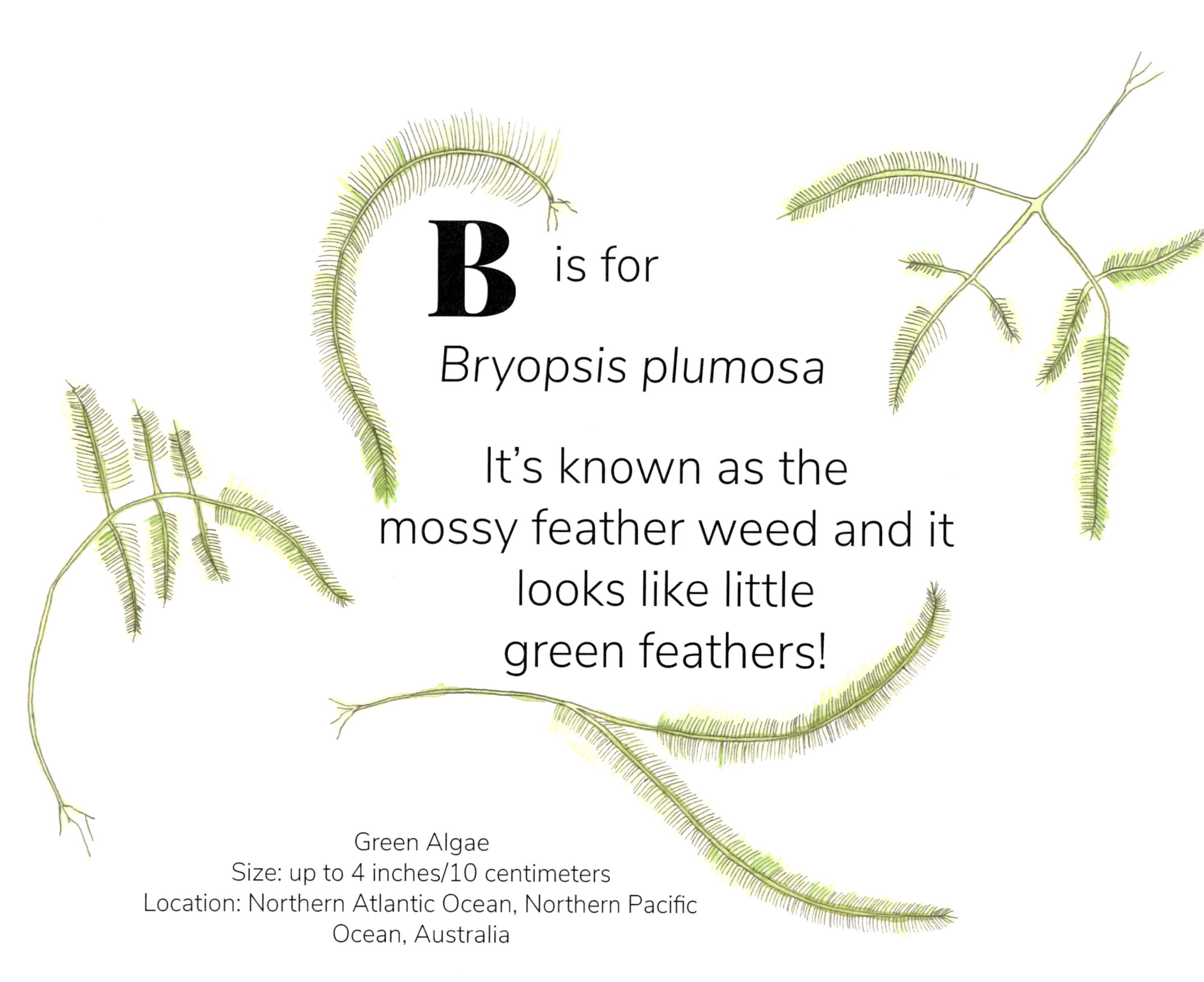

B is for

Bryopsis plumosa

It's known as the mossy feather weed and it looks like little green feathers!

Green Algae
Size: up to 4 inches/10 centimeters
Location: Northern Atlantic Ocean, Northern Pacific Ocean, Australia

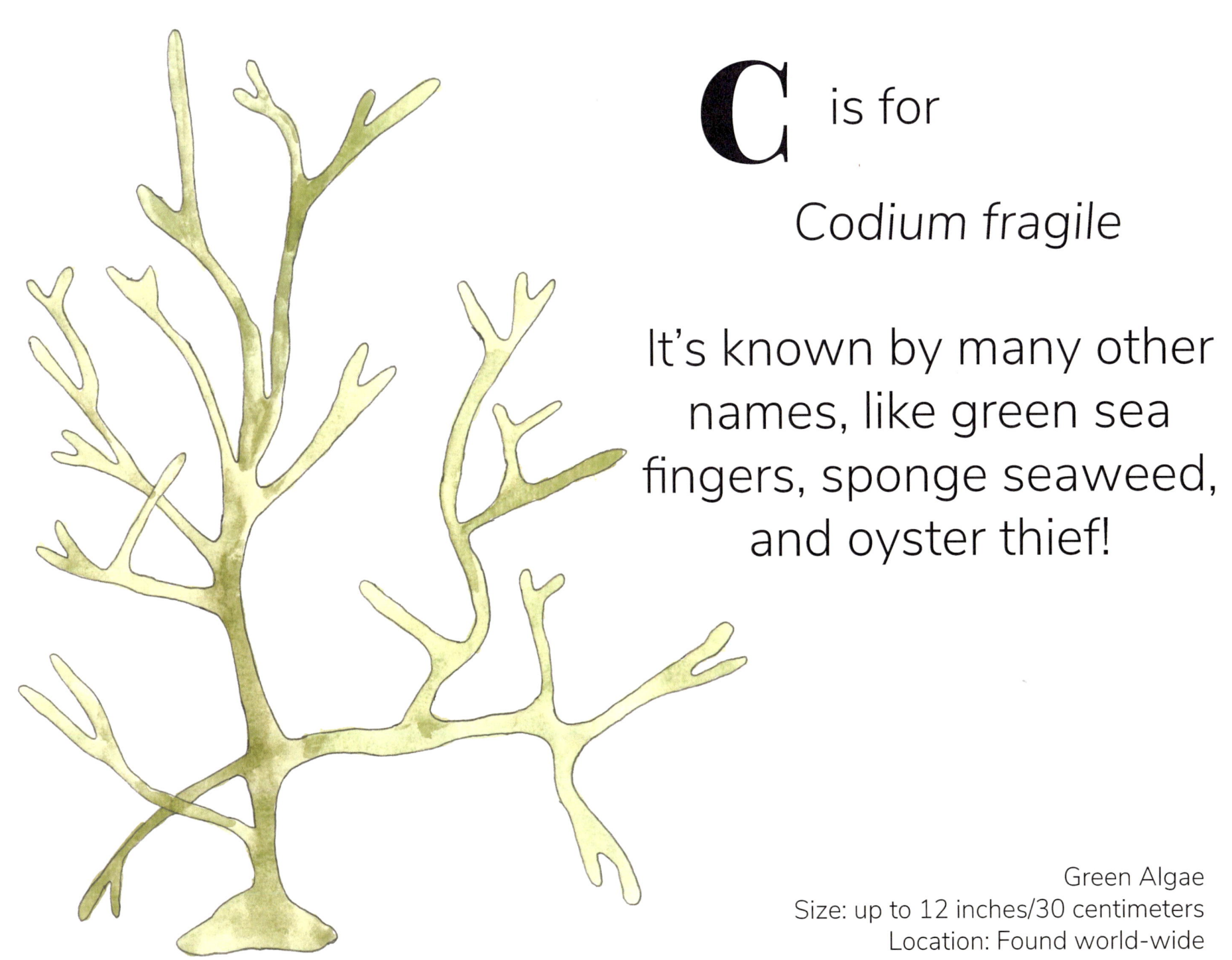

C is for

Codium fragile

It's known by many other names, like green sea fingers, sponge seaweed, and oyster thief!

Green Algae
Size: up to 12 inches/30 centimeters
Location: Found world-wide

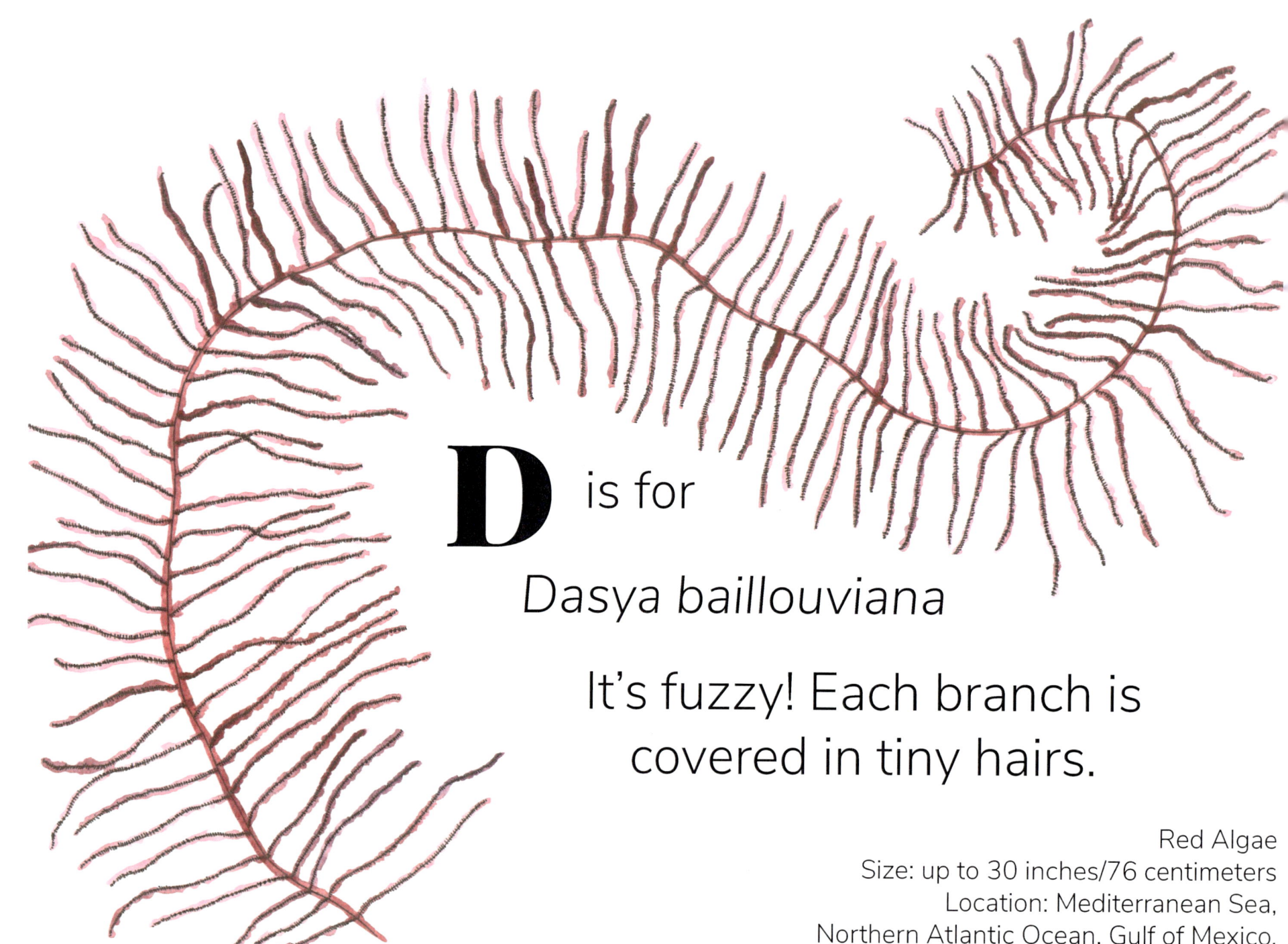

D is for

Dasya baillouviana

It's fuzzy! Each branch is covered in tiny hairs.

Red Algae
Size: up to 30 inches/76 centimeters
Location: Mediterranean Sea, Northern Atlantic Ocean, Gulf of Mexico, Caribbean Sea, Northern Pacific Ocean

E is for *Egregia menziesii*

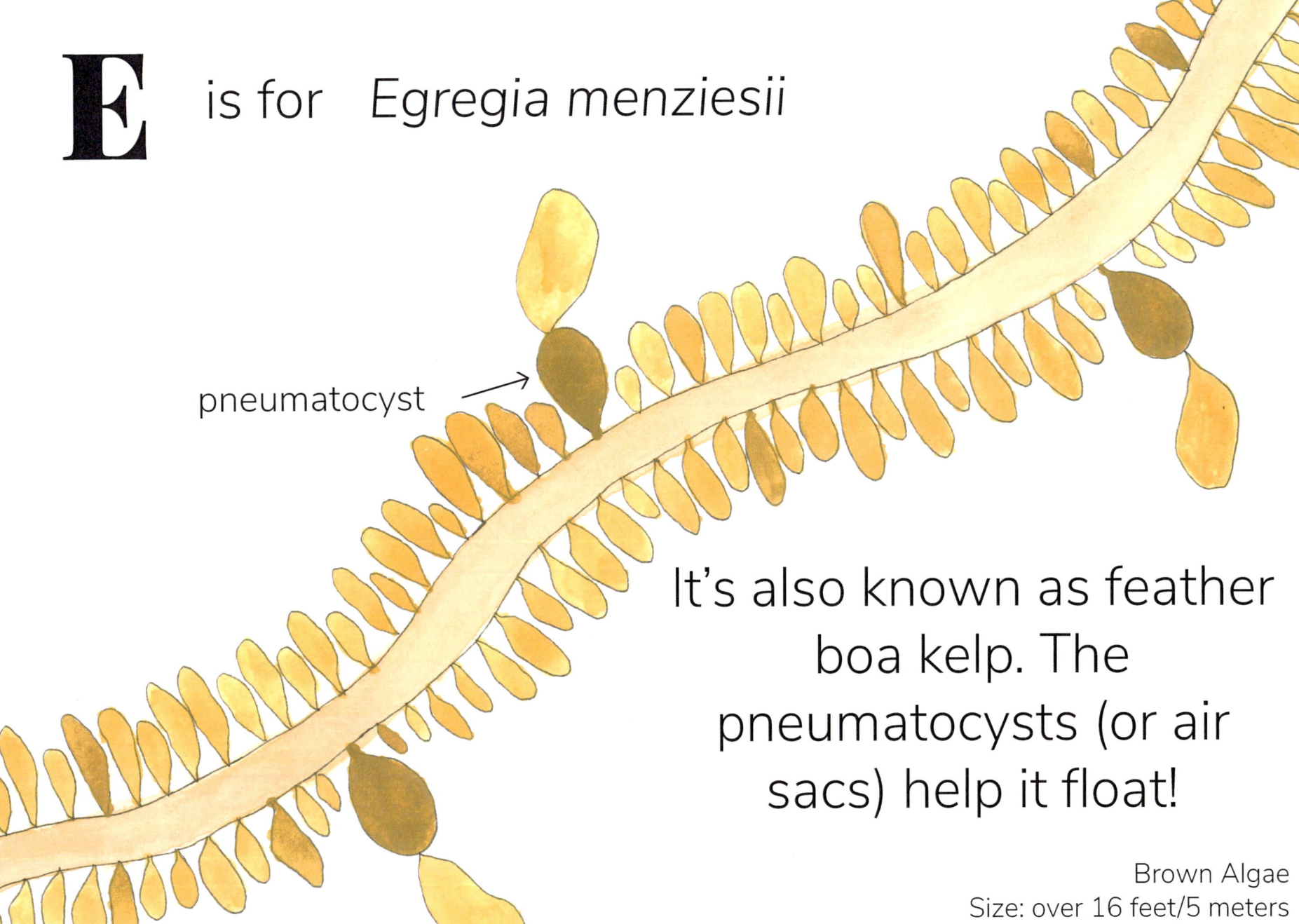

pneumatocyst

It's also known as feather boa kelp. The pneumatocysts (or air sacs) help it float!

Brown Algae
Size: over 16 feet/5 meters
Location: Pacific Ocean from Alaska to Baja California

F is for

Fucus vesiculosus

Also known as bladderwrack and rockweed, it's a home for many animals (especially snails)!

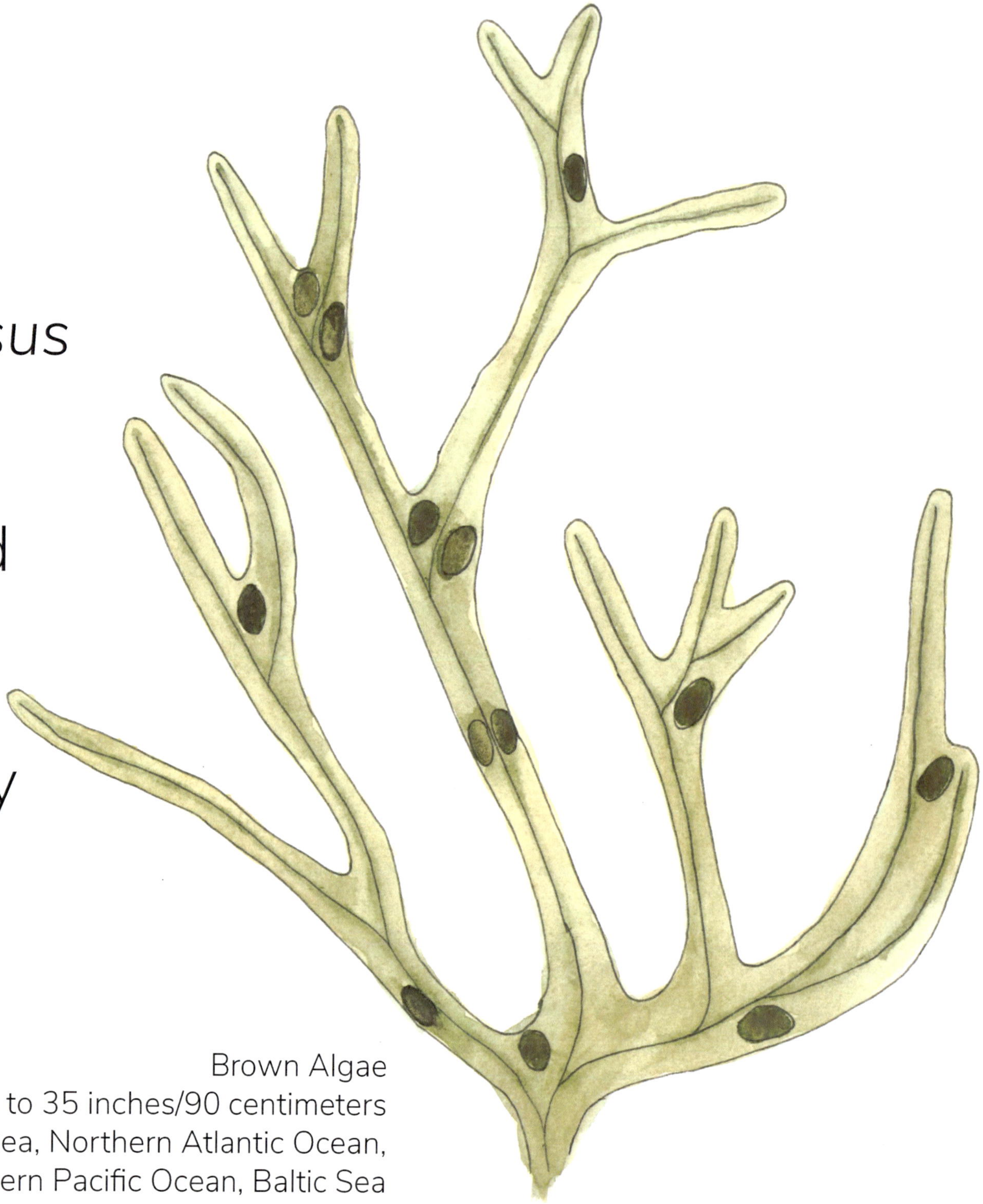

Brown Algae
Size: up to 35 inches/90 centimeters
Location: North Sea, Northern Atlantic Ocean, Northern Pacific Ocean, Baltic Sea

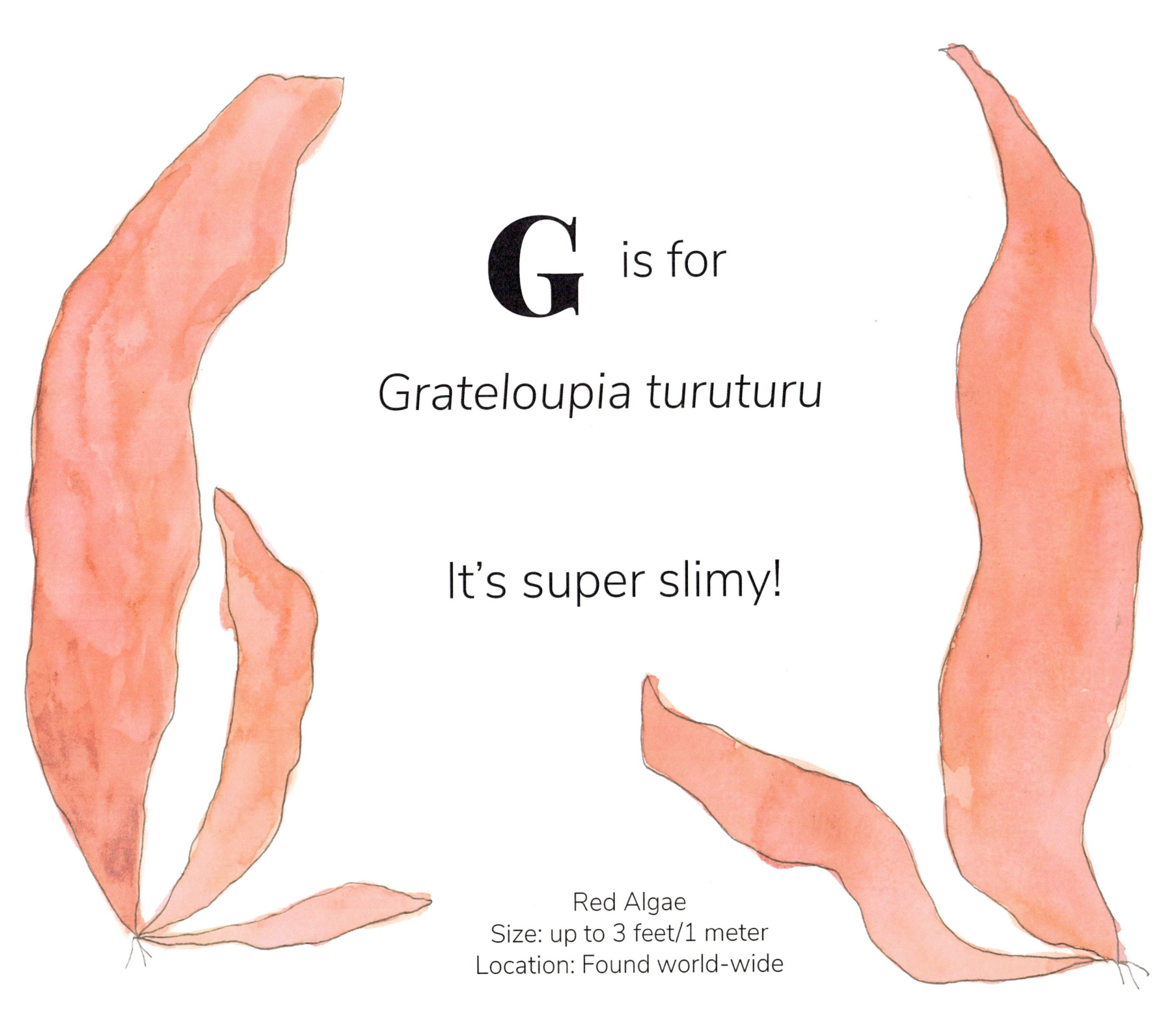

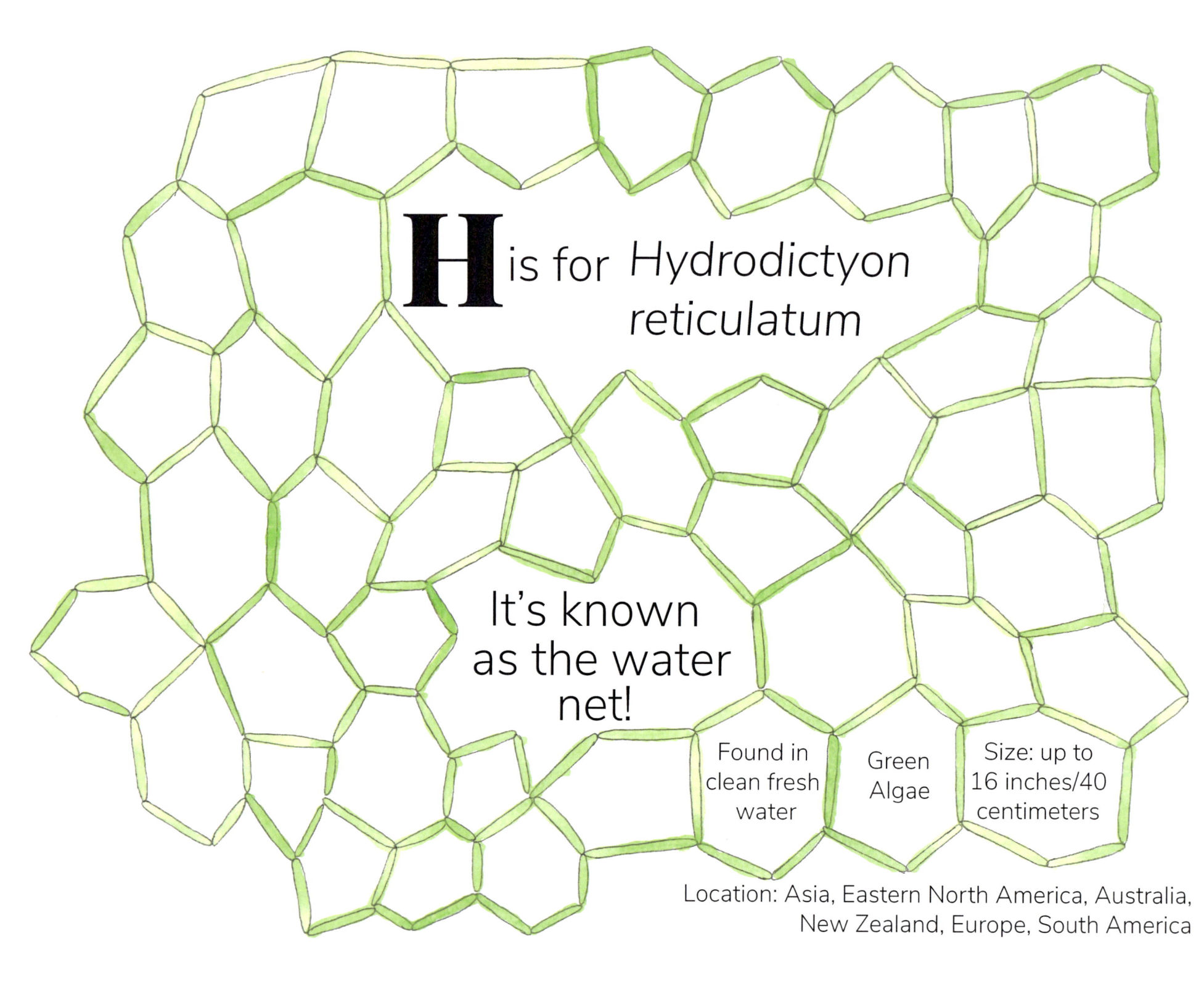

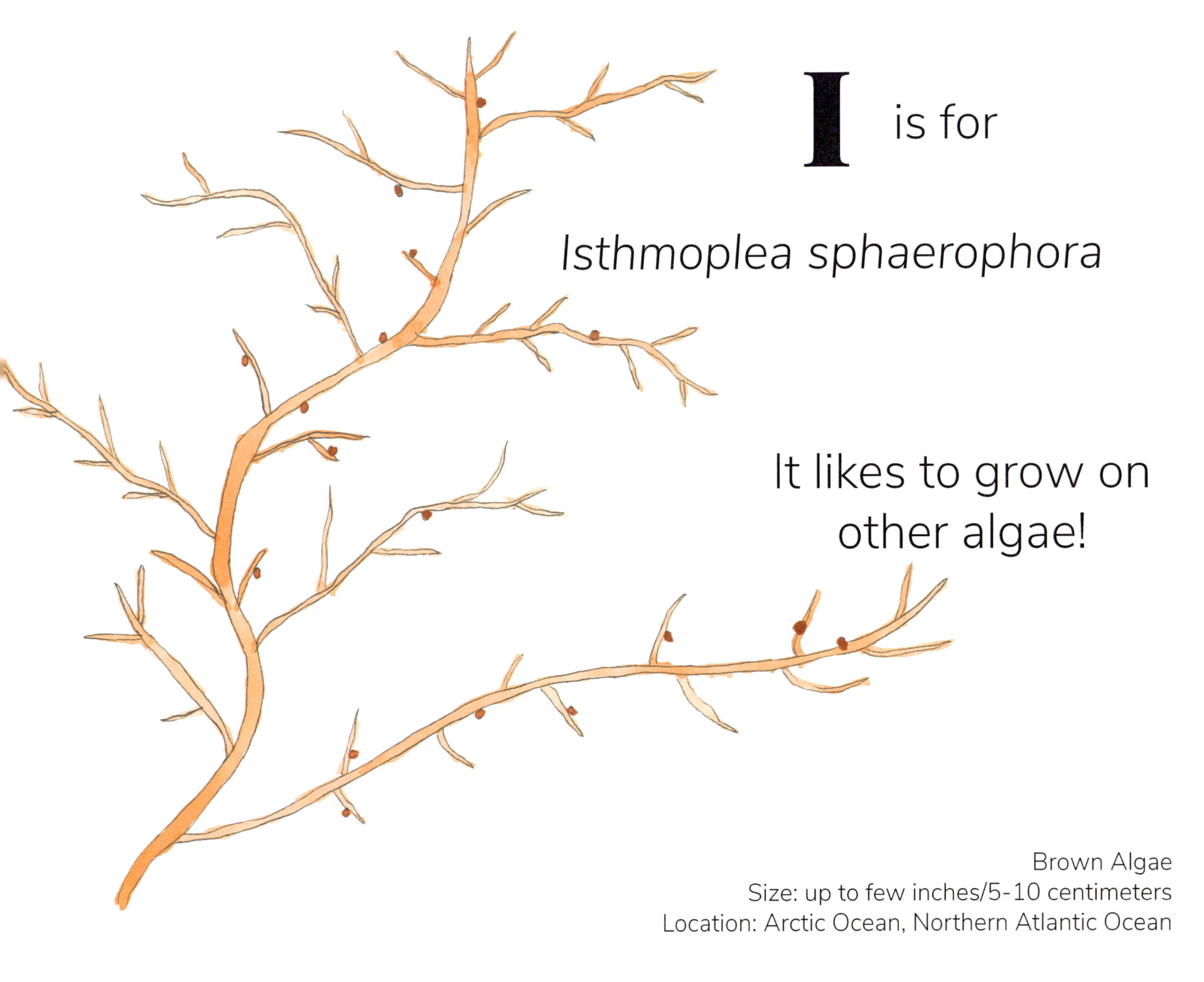

I is for

Isthmoplea sphaerophora

It likes to grow on other algae!

Brown Algae
Size: up to few inches/5-10 centimeters
Location: Arctic Ocean, Northern Atlantic Ocean

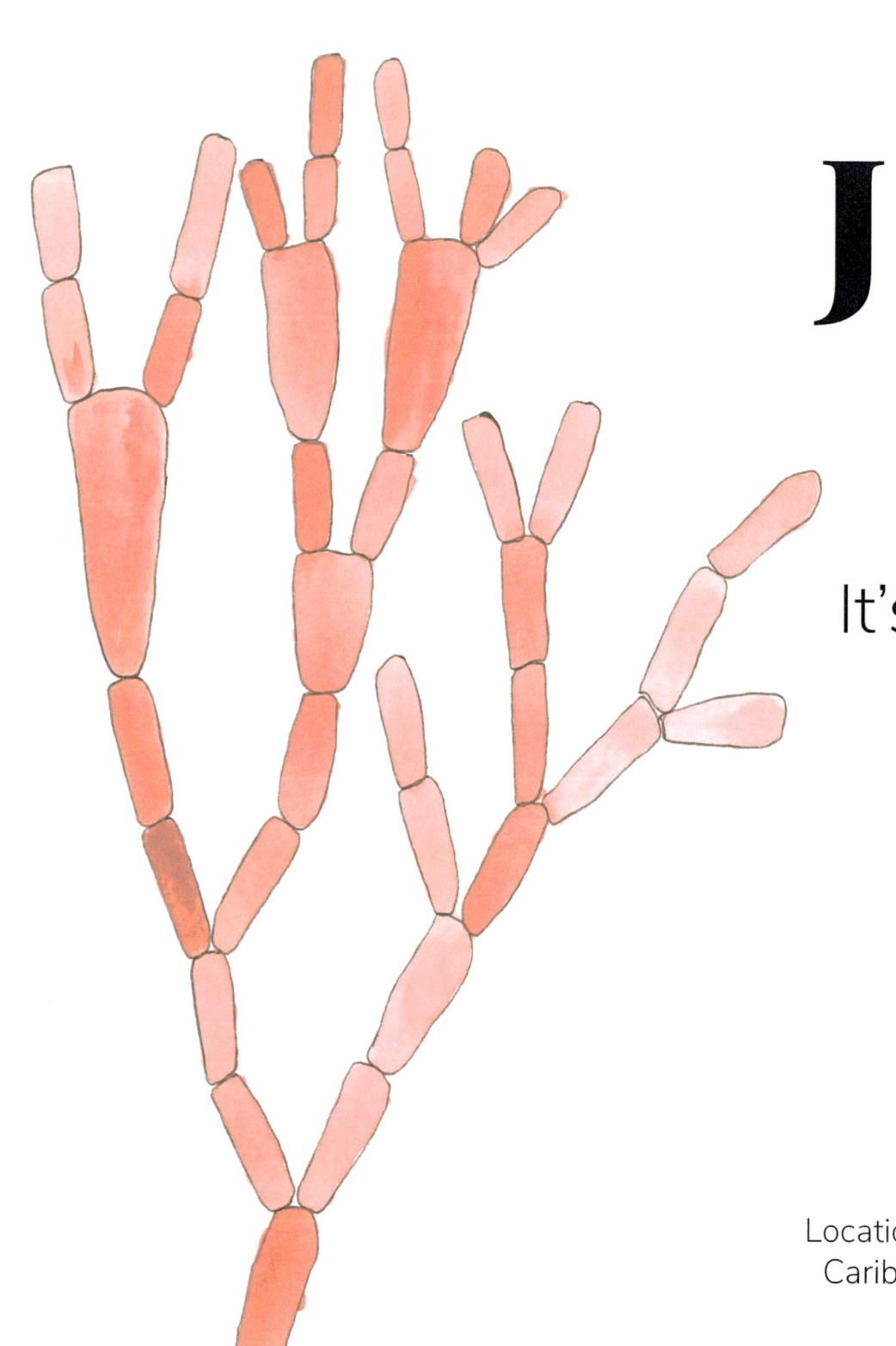

J is for

Jania rubens

It's a crunchy algae - it's made with calcium carbonate
(just like corals)!

Red Algae
Size: up to 2 inches/5 centimeters
Location: Mediterranean Sea, Tropical Atlantic Ocean, Caribbean Sea, Indian Ocean, Tropical Pacific Ocean

K is for *Kallymenia reniformis*

It's also known as kidney weed!

Red Algae
Size: up to 12 inches/30 centimeters long, 7 inches/18 centimeters wide
Location: British Isles, Mediterranean Sea, Northern Atlantic Ocean

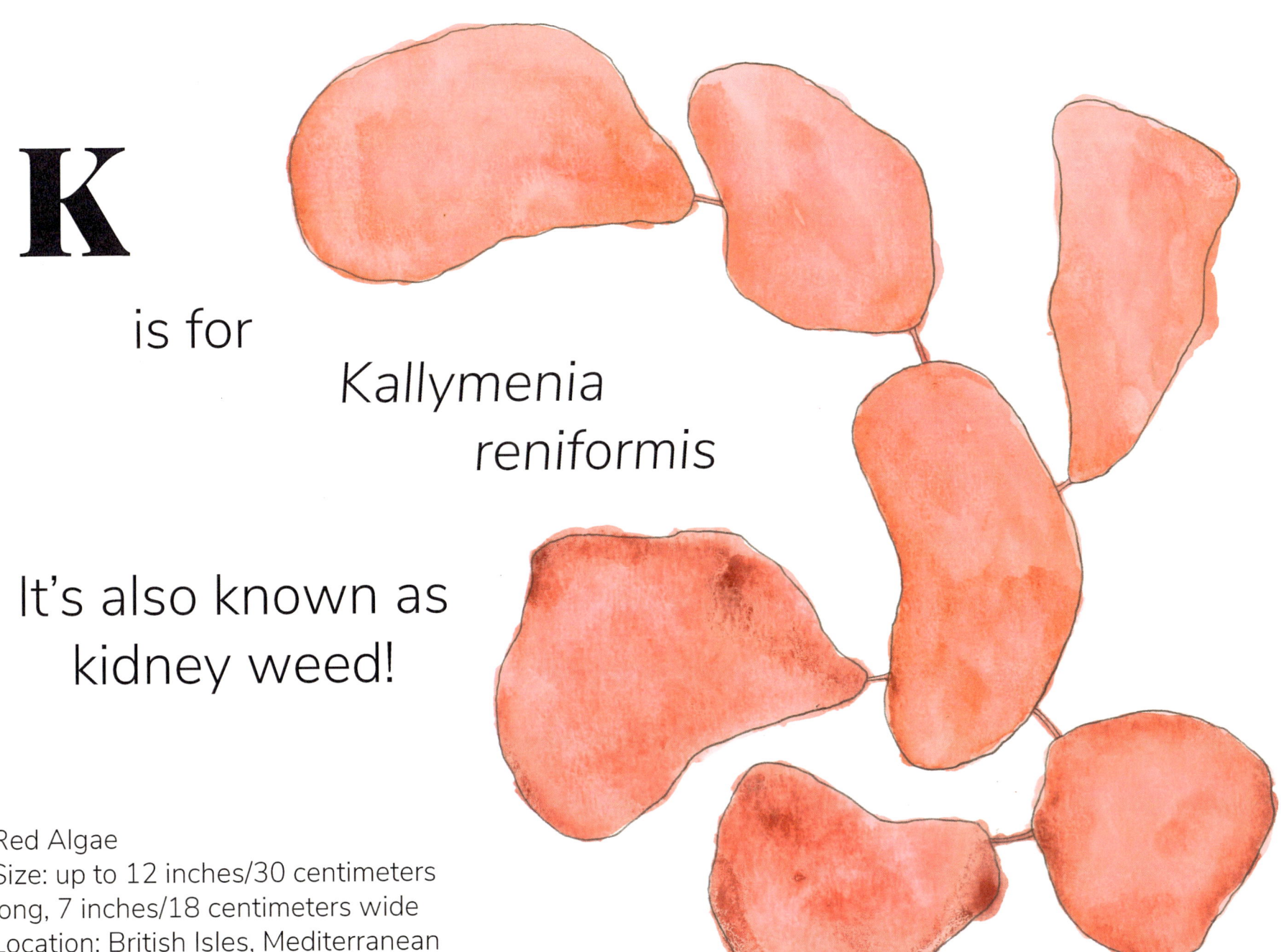

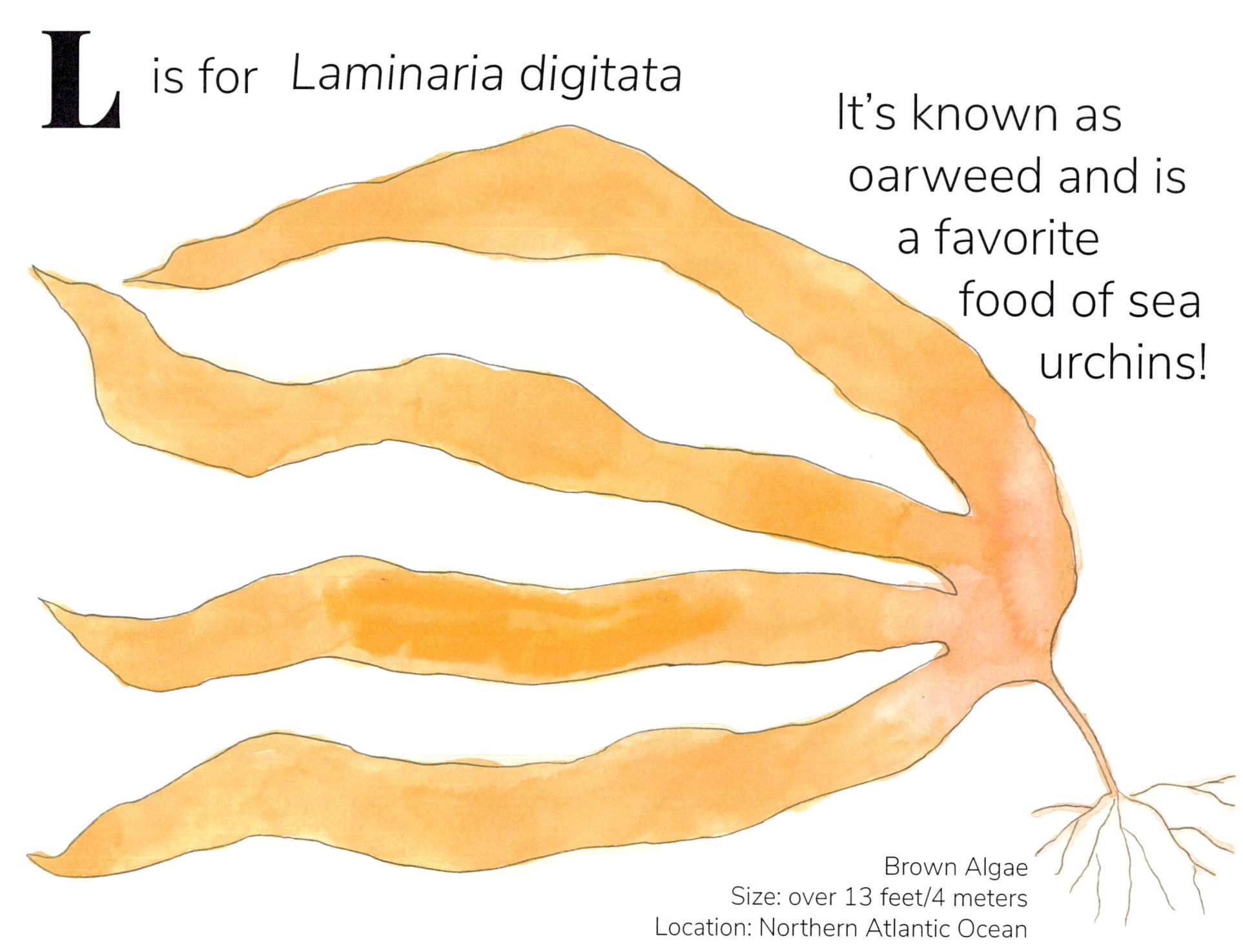

L is for *Laminaria digitata*

It's known as oarweed and is a favorite food of sea urchins!

Brown Algae
Size: over 13 feet/4 meters
Location: Northern Atlantic Ocean

M is for Macrocystis pyrifera

It's known as giant kelp and can grow 22 inches a day! When lots of these grow together, they form a kelp forest where lots of animals like to live.

Brown Algae
Size: over 164 feet/50 meters
Location: Eastern Pacific Ocean, South Africa, New Zealand, Australia

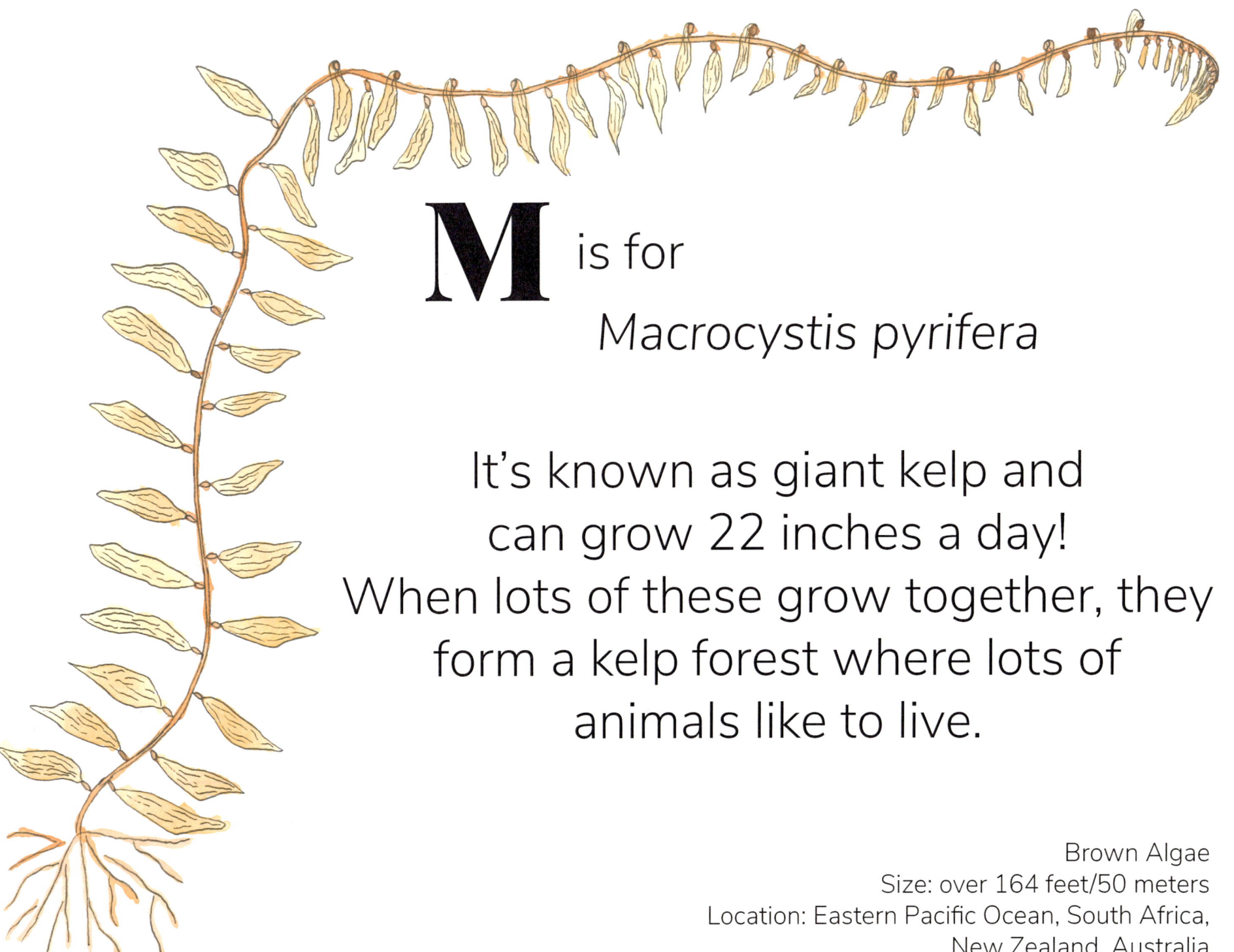

N is for

Nereocystis leutkeana

It's known as bull kelp and ribbon kelp, but its name is Greek for mermaid's bladder!

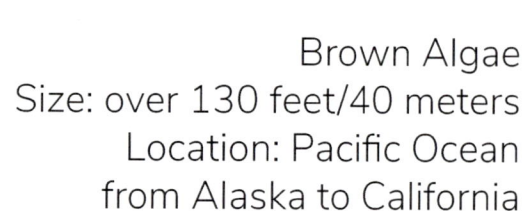

Brown Algae
Size: over 130 feet/40 meters
Location: Pacific Ocean from Alaska to California

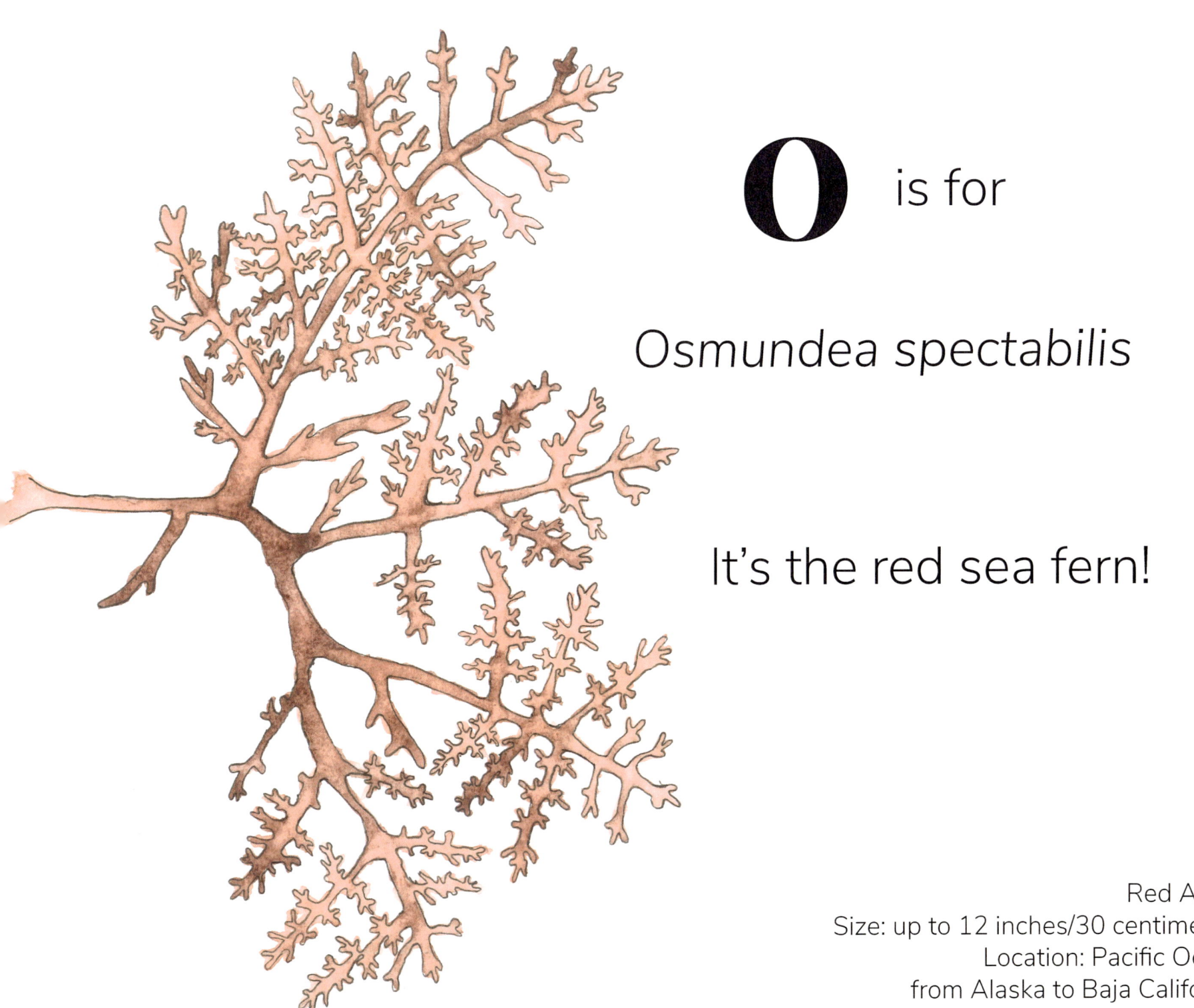

O is for

Osmundea spectabilis

It's the red sea fern!

Red Algae
Size: up to 12 inches/30 centimeters
Location: Pacific Ocean
from Alaska to Baja California

P is for

Porphyra purpurea

It's known as nori and is used for making sushi!

Red Algae
Size: up to 20 inches/50 centimeters
Location: Arctic Ocean, Mediterranean Sea, Northern Atlantic Ocean, Northern Pacific Ocean

Q is for *Quadricoccus verrucosus*

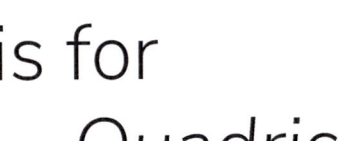
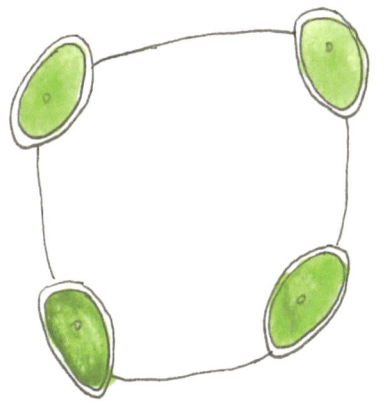
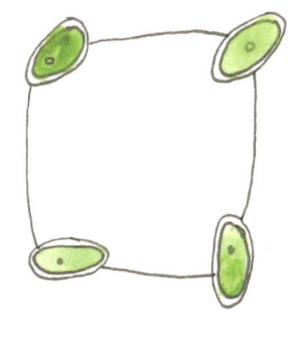

This tiny freshwater algae likes to make little square colonies!

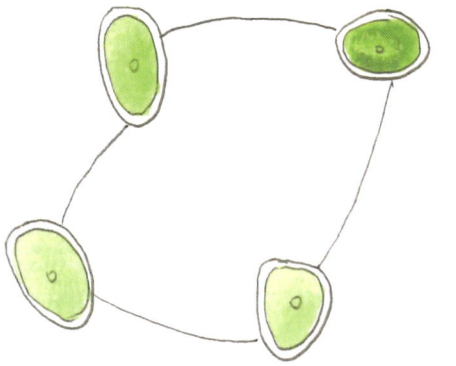
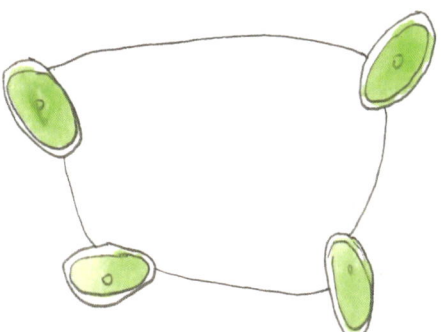

Green Algae
Size: 10 micrometers
(the width of a cotton fiber)
Location: Europe and Asia

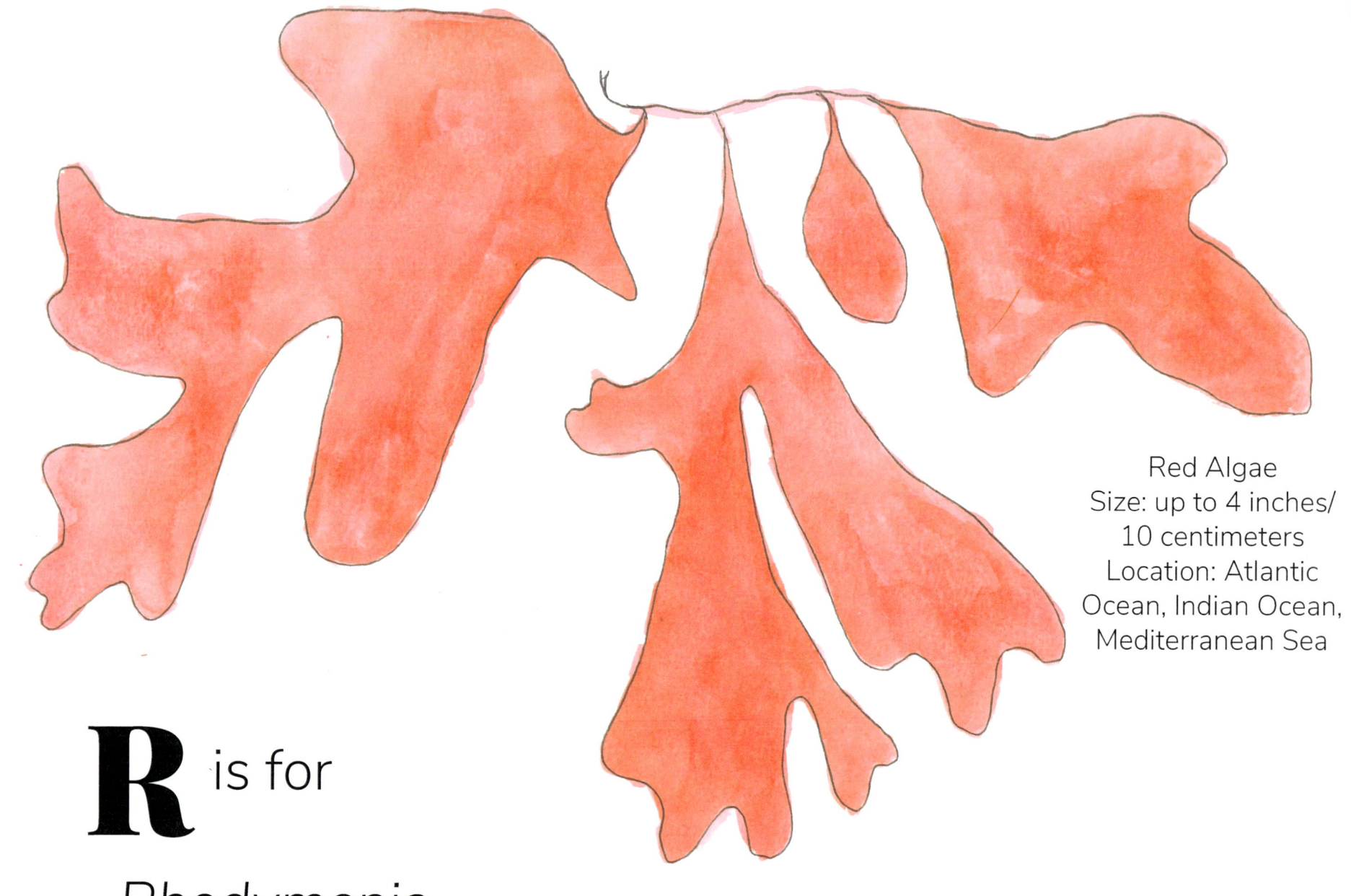

Red Algae
Size: up to 4 inches/ 10 centimeters
Location: Atlantic Ocean, Indian Ocean, Mediterranean Sea

R is for *Rhodymenia pseudopalmata*

It's known as the rosy fan weed!

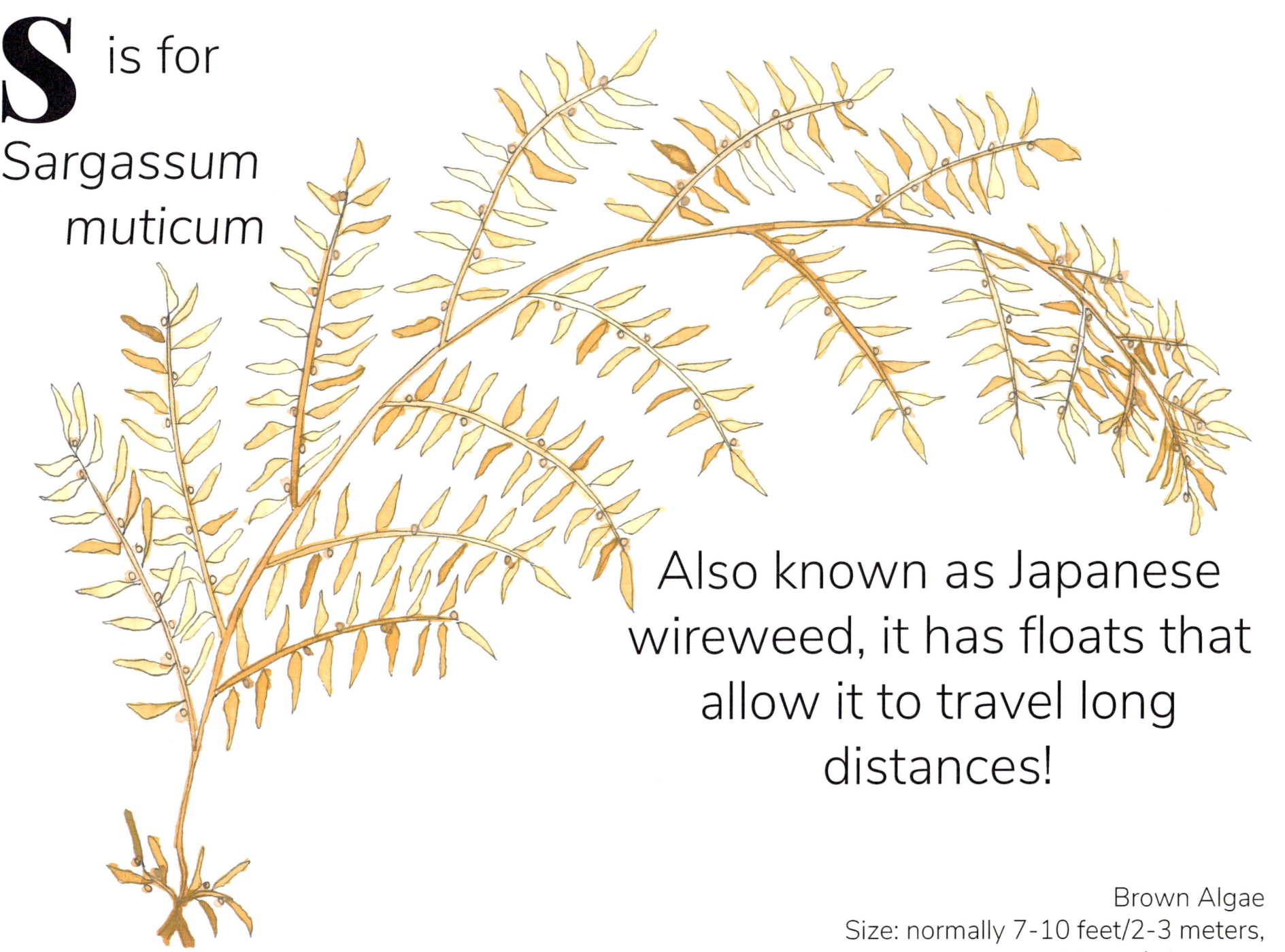

S is for Sargassum muticum

Also known as Japanese wireweed, it has floats that allow it to travel long distances!

Brown Algae
Size: normally 7-10 feet/2-3 meters, but can grow up to 33 feet/10 meters
Location: Found world-wide

T is for Tiffaniella snyderae

In tide pools, it looks like reddish-pink hair!

Red Algae
Size: up to 2 inches/5 centimeters
Location: Eastern Pacific Ocean

U is for

Ulva lactuca

It's known as (and looks like) sea lettuce! Some even put it in soups and salads!

Green Algae
Size: up to 12 inches/30 centimeters
Location: Found world-wide

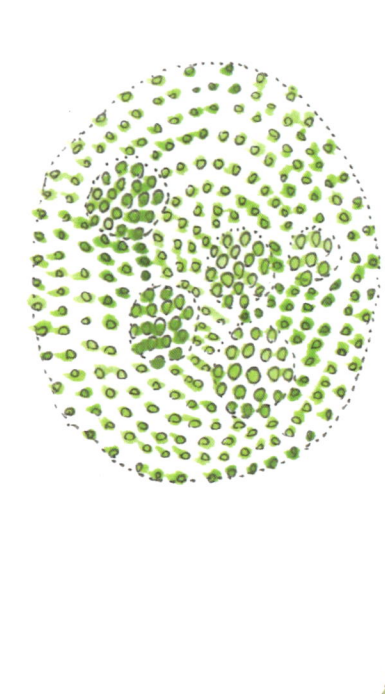

V is for *Volvox aureus*

They can be found in ponds and puddles!

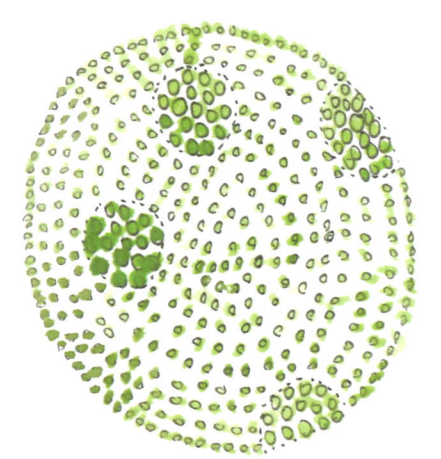
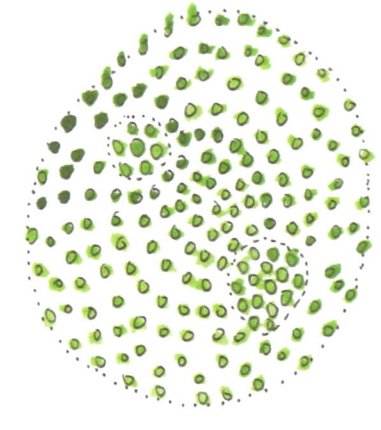

Green Algae
Size: 250 micrometers
(as big as a dust mite)
Location: Found world-wide

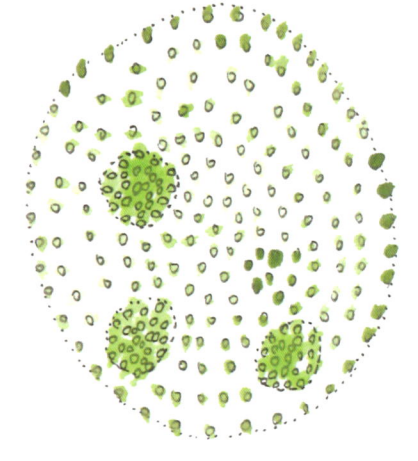

These small freshwater algae form large spherical colonies with 50,000 cells!

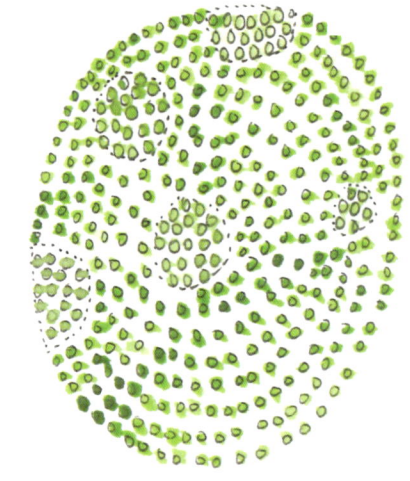

W is for Wildemania amplissima

It's also known as red cellophane because it's only one cell thick and you can see right through it!

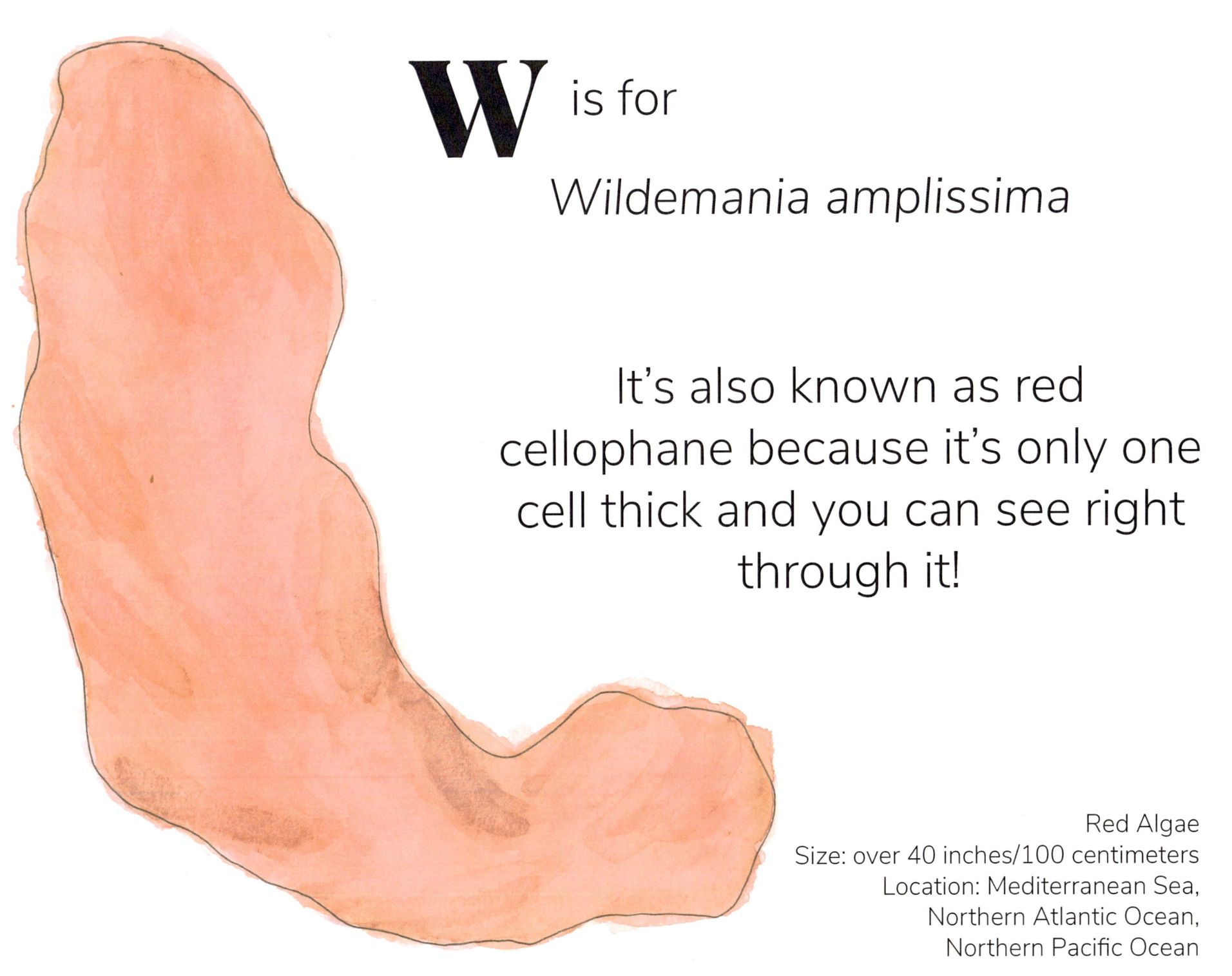

Red Algae
Size: over 40 inches/100 centimeters
Location: Mediterranean Sea, Northern Atlantic Ocean, Northern Pacific Ocean

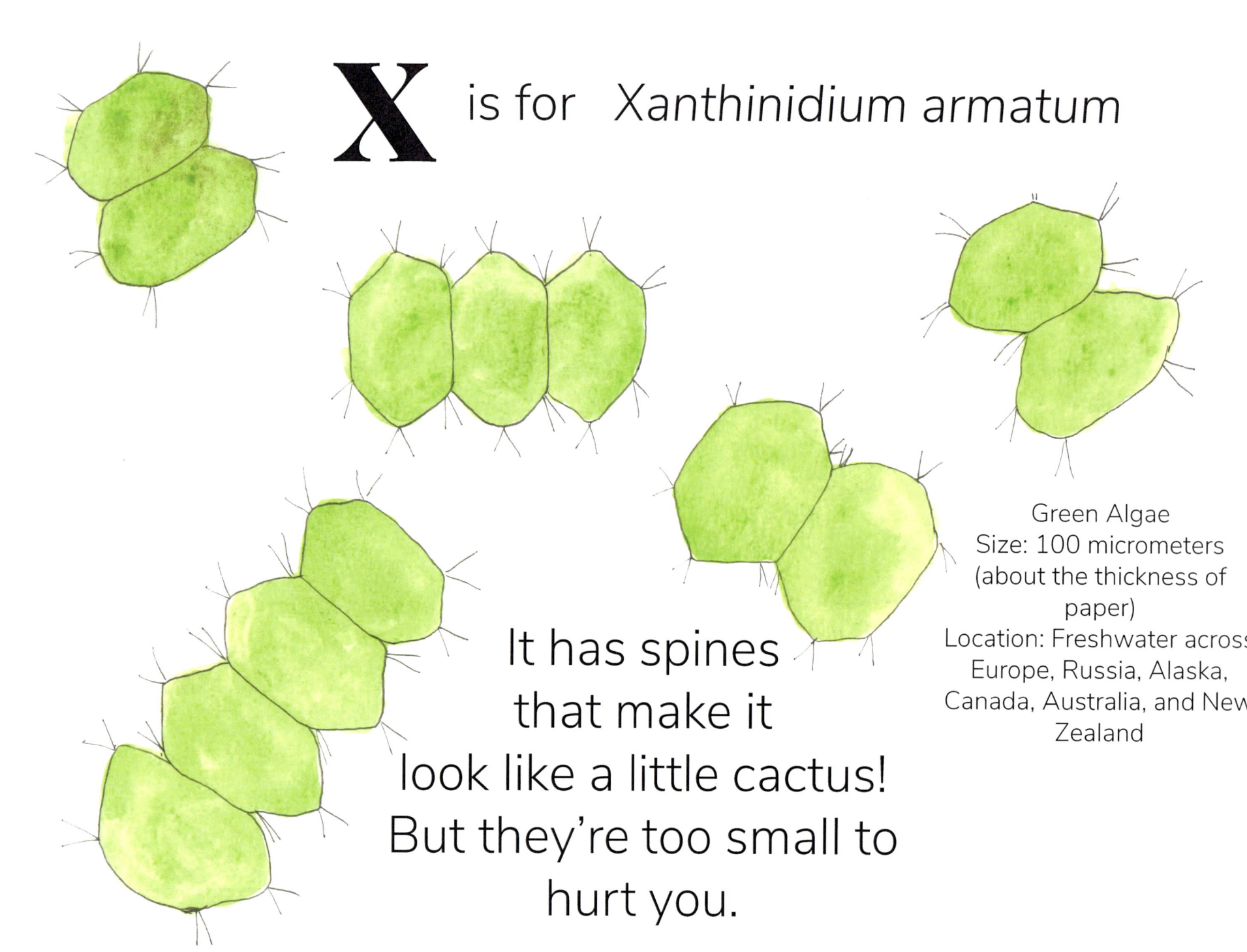

Y is for *Yamadaella grassyi*

It's also made with calcium carbonate (like corals) and lives in the surf zone!

Red Algae
Size: up to 2 inches/5 centimeters
Location: Bermuda

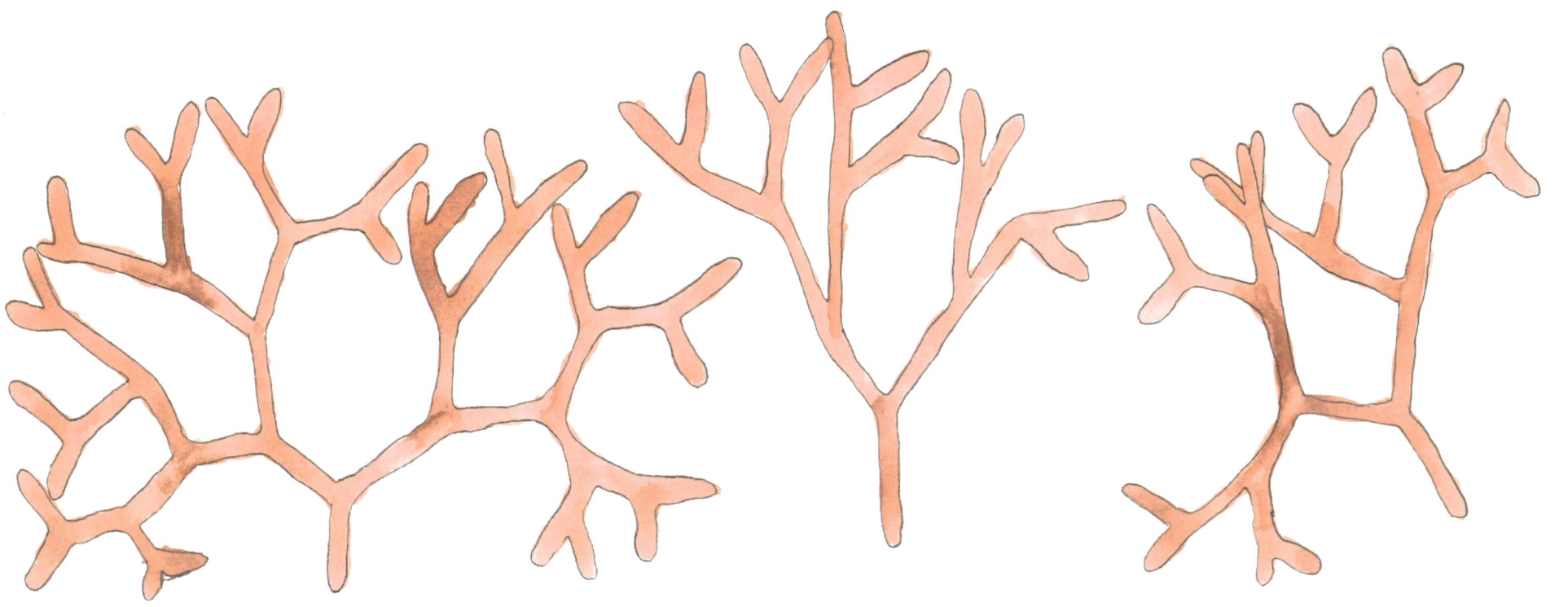

Z is for

Zonaria farlowii

It's also known as the banded tide pool fan!

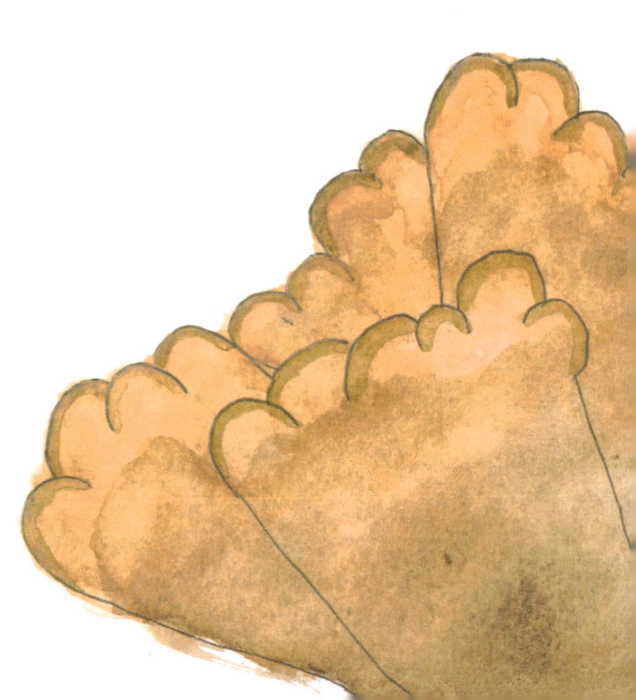

Brown Algae
Size: up to 10 inches/ 25 centimeters
Location: Pacific Ocean from California to Mexico

Pronunciation Guide

Alaria marginata: A-lar-e-uh mar-gin-ah-ta
Bryopsis plumosa: Bry-op-sis plu-mo-sa
Codium fragile: Code-e-um fra-gee-lee
Dasya baillouviana: Day-z-ah bay-lou-vi-ana
Egregia menziesii: E-gre-zhia men-z-z-i
Fucus vesiculosus: Few-cus vuh-sick-u-low-sis
Grateloupia turuturu: Grat-e-loop-e-ah turu-turu
Hydrodictyon reticulatum: Hi-dro-dic-tee-yawn ree-tick-u-lat-um
Isthmoplea sphaerophora: Is-mo-ple-uh s-fair-uh-for-uh
Jania rubens: Jan-e-uh rube-ens
Kallymenia reniformis: Callie-mean-e-uh ren-uh-form-is
Laminaria digitata: Lamb-in-area digit-tata
Macrocystis pyrifera: Macro-cyst-is pie-riff-uh-rah
Nereocystis leutkeana: Near-e-oh-cyst-is lute-key-ana
Osmundea spectabilis: Os-mun-de-uh spec-tab-uh-lis
Porphyra purpurea: Pore-fie-ruh purr-purr-e-uh
Quadricoccus verrucosus: Quad-rah-cah-cus vair-uh-co-sus
Rhodymenia pseudopalmata: Rhody-mean-e-uh sued-o-palm-ata
Sargassum muticum: Sar-gas-sum mute-uh-come
Tiffaniella snyderae: Tif-fan-e-ella snide-er-a
Ulva lactuca: Ole-vah lack-two-cah
Volvox aureus: Vole-vox or-e-us
Wildemania amplissima: Willed-e-main-e-uh amp-lis-sim-uh
Xanthidium armatum: Zan-thid-ium arm-at-um
Yamadaella grassyi: Yam-a-day-ella grass-e-i
Zonaria farlowii: Zone-ar-e-uh far-low-e-i

Front Cover

Saccharina latissima:
    Sack-kah-rhine-uh la-tis-sim-uh
Chondrus crispus:
    Cond-rus crisp-us
Caulpera racemosa:
    Call-per-uh race-mos-uh

Back Cover

Sparlingia pertusa:
    Spar-lin-gee-uh per-two-sa
Ulva intestinalis:
    Ole-vah in-test-tin-al-lis
Costaria costata:
    Co-star-e-uh co-sta-ta

Glossary

Algae: organisms that carry out photosynthesis and generally live in water.

Seaweed: large multicellular algae that live in salt water.

Kelp: large brown seaweeds that typically have high growth rates and a long stalk with a frond divided into strips.
    (for example: *Macrocystis pyrifera* and *Nereocystis leutkeana*)

Red Algae: a large group of algae that includes many seaweeds that are mainly red in color.

Green Algae: a large group of algae and some seaweeds that contain chlorophyll (a pigment that makes them appear green).

Brown Algae: a large group of algae, seaweeds, and kelps, often olive brown or greenish in color.

Photosynthesis: the process by which plants and algae use sunlight to make food from carbon dioxide and water.

Plastid/Chloroplast: an organelle in the cell that contains pigments used in photosynthesis.

Pneumatocyst: a floating structure that contains gas, they provide buoyancy and lift the plant towards the surface.

Epiphyte: an organism that grows on another organism, but is not parasitic.
    (for example: *Isthmoplea sphaerophora*)

Lightning Source UK Ltd.
Milton Keynes UK
UKRC032258250222
399182UK00001B/6